Lean Strategies for Product Development

Achieving Breakthrough Performance in Bringing Products to Market

Also available from ASQ Quality Press:

Lean Enterprise: A Synergistic Approach to Minimizing Waste
William A. Levinson and Raymond A. Rerick

The Change Agent's Guide to Radical Improvement
Ken Miller

Office Kaizen: Transforming Office Operations into a Strategic Competitive Advantage
William Lareau

Customer Centered Six Sigma: Linking Customers, Process Improvement, and Financial Results
Earl Naumann and Steven H. Hoisington

Managing Change: Practical Strategies for Competitive Advantage
Kari Tuominen

The Certified Quality Manager Handbook, Second Edition
Duke Okes and Russell T. Westcott

Root Cause Analysis: Simplified Tools and Techniques
Bjørn Andersen and Tom Fagerhaug

To request a complimentary catalog of ASQ Quality Press publications, call 800-248-1946, or visit our Web site at http://qualitypress.asq.org.

Lean Strategies for Product Development

Achieving Breakthrough Performance in Bringing Products to Market

Clifford Fiore

ASQ Quality Press
Milwaukee, Wisconsin

American Society for Quality, Quality Press, Milwaukee 53203
© 2003 by ASQ
All rights reserved. Published 2003
Printed in the United States of America

12 11 10 09 08 07 06 05 04 03   5 4 3 2 1

Library of Congress Cataloging-in-Publication Data

Fiore, Clifford, 1960–
Lean strategies for product development : achieving breakthrough
performance in bringing products to market / Clifford Fiore.
   p. cm.
Includes bibliographical references and index.
ISBN 0-87389-604-1 (pbk. ; alk. paper)
1. New products—Management. 2. Industrial efficiency. 3. Industrial
procurement—Management. I. Title.

HF5415.153.F4 2003
658.5'75—dc21   2003013780

ISBN 0-87389-604-1

Publisher: William A. Tony
Acquisitions Editor: Annemieke Hytinen
Project Editor: Paul O'Mara
Production Administrator: Gretchen Trautman
Special Marketing Representative: David Luth

ASQ Mission: The American Society for Quality advances individual,
organizational, and community excellence worldwide through learning,
quality improvement, and knowledge exchange.

Attention Bookstores, Wholesalers, Schools, and Corporations: ASQ Quality
Press books, videotapes, audiotapes, and software are available at quantity
discounts with bulk purchases for business, educational, or instructional use.
For information, please contact ASQ Quality Press at 800-248-1946, or write to
ASQ Quality Press, P.O. Box 3005, Milwaukee, WI 53201-3005.

To place orders or to request a free copy of the ASQ Quality Press Publications
Catalog, including ASQ membership information, call 800-248-1946. Visit our
Web site at www.asq.org or http://qualitypress.asq.org.

 Printed on acid-free paper

American Society for Quality

Quality Press
600 N. Plankinton Avenue
Milwaukee, Wisconsin 53203
Call toll free 800-248-1946
Fax 414-272-1734
www.asq.org
http://qualitypress.asq.org
http://standardsgroup.asq.org
E-mail: authors@asq.org

To my wife Deidre,
and my sons Kendall, Donovan, and Bradley

Table of Contents

Acknowledgments

Throughout my professional career, I've been blessed with the opportunity to work with many talented and wonderful people. The willingness of these individuals, too numerous to name, to share their expertise and experiences taught me invaluable lessons for which I am eternally grateful. Unbeknownst to them, the experiences and knowledge I gained from these individuals were a significant contribution in helping me write this book.

Secondly, I wish to extend a special note of gratitude to Dale Jensen, my mentor and former manager, whose guidance and shared vision in the area of lean concepts and product development were major influences in the creation of this book.

Finally, I wish to acknowledge the true guiding lights of my life: my parents, who have been the biggest influence in my life and instilled in me the virtues of trying my best and seeking new challenges, and my wife Deidre, and sons Kendall, Donovan, and Bradley, who in my eyes represent the true joys and celebration of life.

Preface

The pressure to be profitable facing companies has never been greater than it is today. With the intense competition that exists in today's business environment, the key discriminator for the most successful companies is the ability to provide products to the marketplace quickly and cheaply. Consequently, the "lifeblood" of many companies rests in the product development processes that enable a company to provide a continual stream of new products that are better, cheaper, and reach the customer faster than the competition. In conjunction with this objective, there has been in recent years an emergence and application of lean concepts to further generate a competitive advantage. While considerable literature is available regarding the application of lean concepts within manufacturing and production arenas, very little information is available in applying these concepts in the area of product development and to a greater extent, other nonmanufacturing related disciplines. *Lean Strategies for Product Development* was created to fill that void.

Lean Strategies highlights problems that are common to companies in terms of developing products cheaply and efficiently. In response, this volume represents one of the first books in the industry to couple the proven concepts of lean with engineering processes dealing with product development. The result is a book based on proven strategies and methodologies that will enable a company to significantly reduce the time necessary to develop new products and dramatically reduce product cost. The concepts are presented in the context of a story centered on two key characters—a customer and his supplier. Through the dialog shared between the characters, the concepts are presented and a new business opportunity emerges.

Companies that have implemented the concepts presented in *Lean Strategies for Product Development* have achieved dramatic results. In some cases, cycle time reduction by as much as 70 percent has been achieved! It was the interest generated from these results and the desire by others to replicate this methodology that provided the basis for writing *Lean Strategies for Product Development*. The goal was to create a concise, easy-to-read book that would clearly convey concepts and benefits that others could replicate. My hope is that you will enjoy reading *Lean Strategies for Product Development* not only for the story line, but also for gaining an understanding of the key concepts that are presented. With reductions in product development cycle time and reduced cost, you will reap rewards through a competitive advantage that will ultimately make your business enterprise significantly more profitable.

Clifford Fiore

1

Customer Visit

Brad Connelly glanced at his watch as he entered the lobby of Donetics Industries. He was a few minutes early for his 8:00 AM meeting with Ken Hawkins. After signing in, he settled down in a chair, placing his briefcase beside him. For Brad, this was another routine business trip to check up on some technical and production issues with a supplier. As a program manager for Terra Solutions Inc., he had considerable experience in working with suppliers.

Terra Solutions is a conglomerate specializing in the design and manufacture of farm tractors, harvesters, lawn mowers, and other household lawn and garden machines. Brad is a 17-year veteran of the company, having started out in the design group as a mechanical engineer straight out of college. Over the years, he successfully climbed the corporate ladder, taking on various jobs in engineering and operations. For the last three years, Brad has been heading up the Atlas program— a full line of commercial and residential-grade lawn mowers produced by Terra Solutions. Although by nature more comfortable in dealing with technical issues, he had nonetheless earned his stripes as a successful program manager by developing a keen understanding of the business end of the job. A hard and conscientious worker, he was sensitive to how he was perceived by others in the organization. Brad took pride in the fact that colleagues viewed him as a down-to-earth guy who really knew his stuff.

Donetics Industries is a leading supplier in the manufacture of electric motors, generators, gas-powered engines, and hydraulic pump systems. Their products are used in a variety of industries, including household appliances, lawn and garden equipment, power tools, and heavy construction equipment. Most recently, the company expanded its customer base to include lift systems for roller coasters and amusement park rides.

Ken Hawkins is the project engineer for the gas-powered engine that Donetics produces for the Atlas program. He has been associated with the project since its inception almost three years ago. Since the development phase of the project, Brad and Ken have spent considerable time together and developed a friendly business relationship. During business trips, they would invite each other to their homes for dinner, and shared common interests in sports, books, and traveling.

Brad's trip to Donetics was intended to serve two purposes. First, to address a potential problem with the engine throttle. During a routine check of some production units, Terra Solutions discovered indications of excessive spring wear. Although not an immediate problem, Brad was concerned about the long-term effects of this condition since Atlas mower production was going to ramp up considerably over the next few months. The trip would allow Ken and Donetics an opportunity to review data provided by Brad in order to come up with a game plan to address the issue. Second, in light of the production ramp-up, Brad wanted to meet with Ken's Operations people to discuss the production schedule for the upcoming six months.

Brad glanced again at his watch. It was now 8:03 AM. Just then the adjoining door to the lobby swung open. It was Ken Hawkins. Quickly scanning the lobby, Ken's eyes fixed on his guest. "Brad, there you are. How are you doing?" Before he could reply, Ken continued. "Sorry I'm running a few minutes late. I just finished up with a customer on the phone and got down here as quickly as I could."

"That's okay, no problem at all," replied Brad as he stood up and shook Ken's hand. "I was just sitting here relaxing for a few minutes."

"Oh, did you have a rough trip coming down here?" asked Ken.

"No, not really," said Brad. "The kids and I just got back from a quick camping trip to the mountains. I thought it would be a chance to kick back and relax, but they keep me on the go so much, I was more tired when I got back than when I left!"

"I can relate to that," chuckled Ken.

"How about you, Ken? How are things going for you?" asked Brad.

"Everything is fine. The family is doing well. The kids have been keeping me really busy lately with all of their school activities. Between soccer, the Girl Scouts, and band practices, I have a hard time keeping on top of where I need to be each day after work. But seriously, though, it's a lot of fun."

"Glad to hear that," stated Brad.

"So are you ready to get down to business?" asked Ken, "I've got a conference room already lined up for us."

"Sounds good," replied Brad. "First I'd like to review the throttle spring wear issue with you. During lunch, I made arrangements to have a short meeting with Traci Donovan from your Operations department to discuss the production schedule. As you know, the Atlas schedule picks up in the next few months. After finishing up with her, we can reconvene this afternoon to tie up any loose ends with the spring issue. Does that sound okay to you?"

"Sounds like a plan to me," said Ken. "Let's go down to the conference room."

2

New Competition

It was 11:33 AM when Brad looked at his watch. "Well, Ken, I think we've put together a pretty good plan to address the throttle problem. To summarize, you are going to increase the wire size to improve the spring life and I'm going to perform some additional testing to confirm the vibration requirements for the engine mounts and cable connections. Barring any unforeseen issues from the test data, I think this will solve our problem."

"I agree, Brad," replied Ken. "I think this is a good approach."

"What do you say about taking a break for lunch?" suggested Brad as he opened up his briefcase and began looking for something. "I'd like to have that quick meeting with Traci, and then you and I can get together after lunch to finalize some of the dates for these action items."

"That will work for me," exclaimed Ken. "I'll get a bite to eat and take care of a few things around the office. Would you like to meet again, oh, say, around one o'clock?"

Totally distracted by searching through his briefcase, without looking up Brad responded, "One is fine."

"I can't seem to find the copy of the updated production schedule I wanted to give Traci," he mumbled.

Becoming increasingly perplexed, Brad began placing items from his briefcase all around him on the table. Finally, he exclaimed, "Here it is!" and raised the document up as if it was a fly that he had snatched right out of the air. "I thought I'd lost this."

As Brad began putting the items back into his briefcase, Ken noticed a brochure with a picture of a gas-powered engine with an electric starter. "That's an interesting product," he stated, referring to the brochure in a most inquisitive manner.

"Oh, you're referring to the engine with the electric starter," replied Brad, as he picked up the brochure and handed it to Ken. "You see, after we finish up here, I'm going to visit this supplier to learn more about their product."

"Oh, I see," replied Ken.

"With the popularity of the Atlas mowers," continued Brad, as he put the last item back in his briefcase, "we're already in the planning stages for the next product spin-off. Part of our strategy for the new product is to integrate some new features that we've developed since the inception of the current model. Also, we want to do this without increasing cost, and to introduce the product into the market as soon as we can. We see a window of opportunity here that we don't want to miss out on."

"So how does the electric-starting engine fit into this?" inquired Ken. "If you don't mind me asking."

"No, not at all," replied Brad. "I don't have a lot of detail, but this supplier has a proven track record of short cycle times in developing their products. Also, the cost is competitive with manual-starting engines. In terms of their technology, I'm not *that* familiar with the electric version compared to the manual ones we've been using, but I'm going to find out."

"So let me get this straight," interjected Ken. "What you're telling me is that you're considering using an electric-starting engine in your new mower model even though you've *never* used one before?"

"That's right, Ken. Like I said, we have a window of opportunity here we don't want to pass up, so it's an option we're going to look in to."

"Have you considered using a Donetics manual-starting engine for your new lawn mower?" asked Ken. "After all, our product is on the current model. Doesn't our track record speak for itself?"

"To be perfectly frank with you, Ken, it's because of your track record that we are considering other options," retorted Brad. "Donetics has a history of providing good products that meet our needs. But, from our point of view, your products cost too much and take too long to bring to market. In recent years, some of your products that we use on other programs took over a year to develop! With our goals for the new lawn mower model, we just can't afford that level of performance from Donetics."

"I see your point, Brad," admitted Ken. "Actually, you're not the first customer to tell us that. I asked the question because I wanted to make sure I clearly understood your position. Have you determined what the requirements are for the new engine?"

"Actually, we have," replied Brad. "Take a look at this," he continued, as he handed a copy of a data sheet to Ken. "It should be pretty familiar to you. It contains the same basic information that you've seen in the past for other programs. I'm going to use this information as a basis for discussion with the other supplier. You can keep that copy if you like."

"Yes, it looks pretty familiar," confirmed Ken as he quickly scanned the material. "Thanks for the copy, Brad." Quickly changing the subject as he stood up to exit the conference room, he added, "So, I'd better let you go to your meeting with Traci. I'll meet you back here at one o'clock."

"Okay. See you in a little while," replied Brad.

3

Creating an Opportunity

It was shortly before one o'clock when Ken reentered the conference room. Brad had arrived just a moment before. "Oh no, I hope you haven't been waiting too long this time," exclaimed Ken.

"No, not at all," chuckled Brad. "I got here just before you did."

"At least I wasn't late this time," replied Ken in a relieved voice. "How was your meeting with Traci?"

"It went well," said Brad. "We reviewed the schedule and came up with a plan to meet the increased demand. I think it will work out fine."

"Before we get started again and talk about milestones, I have something for you," said Ken as he opened up a folder he had brought with him. He handed Brad a CD-ROM disc and a computer generated graphic plot of a gas-powered engine.

"What's this?" asked Brad.

"It's a Donetics proposal for a manual-starting gas-powered engine on your new Atlas lawn mower," declared Ken.

"What?"

"It's a proposal for the engine on your new lawn mower," repeated Ken.

"You mean the one we were discussing before lunch?" questioned Brad. "You mean to tell me that within an hour and a half you've come up with a concept for the new engine?" he continued. "I don't believe it. I really don't believe it."

"It's true," responded Ken. "Based on the data sheet you provided, this is what we believe will work for you. In addition to the plot, the CD-ROM contains a computer-aided design (CAD) mock-up model you can plug into your design at Terra Solutions to do some fit checks."

"Hang on a minute, Ken," Brad said incredulously. "I know you, I know your company, and I know your track record, and there's no way you can come in here and tell me you've put together a concept in an hour and a half."

"Well, up until the last few months, that would have been a very true statement," rebutted Ken. "But we've been working on some things over the past year to improve our performance."

"So what you're telling me is that this is a real concept?" replied Brad, holding up the computer plot. "This is on the up-and-up?"

"Yeah," replied Ken innocently.

"Well, I'd really like to know how you've been able to do this," stated Brad.

"Do you have time?" asked Ken.

"My flight doesn't leave until later tonight. It won't take us that long to finalize the milestones for the spring issue. Besides, I would much rather stay here and understand how you've pulled this off rather than sitting around an airport terminal waiting for my flight," mused Brad.

"Okay," responded Ken. "Why don't we first get some coffee and then I'll answer all of the questions you have?"

"Sounds good to me," replied Brad.

4

Lean Concepts

"**B**rad, remember earlier when I asked if you had considered using our engine for your new lawn mower?" asked Ken. "Then, after you gave me your answer I told you that was not the first time we had heard that?"

Brad nodded.

"Well," Ken continued, "I must confess, I kind of set you up with that question."

"What do you mean?" responded Brad.

"I knew exactly what you were going to say," confessed Ken. "The reality is that some of our customers, actually, *many* of our customers, have been telling us exactly the same things that you described as our problems. And we've been hearing it for quite a while now.

"Up until very recently, we were losing new business opportunities at an alarming rate," continued Ken. "Many of our customers told us that we presented a good product, but it cost too much or that we couldn't meet the schedule. We were quickly losing the leadership position and market share it took us years to develop! Finally, we got the message. We realized we were victims of our own inefficiencies. We realized that if we didn't change our way of doing business, we wouldn't be around much longer!"

"So what did you do?" inquired Brad.

"Let me respond to that question by asking you a question," declared Ken. "Brad, are you familiar with 'lean manufacturing' principles?" he asked.

"Yeah," replied Brad. "I can give you the definition of what lean is from the training I received at Terra Solutions. Lean is producing what is needed, when it is needed, with the minimum amount of resources and space. We've had some pretty good success in applying lean concepts in our final assembly areas. But how does that relate to what we're discussing here?"

"Same with us," added Ken. "We started, oh, about four years ago in our manufacturing area. We created lean cells that were responsible for manufacturing the parts. In addition, we were able to standardize work processes, reduce inventory levels, and eliminate a lot of waste."

"I still don't see the tie-in," interjected Brad.

"Well," continued Ken, "we made some really good improvements using these concepts. But when we took a closer look at the quality issues that we were continually dealing with in the manufacturing cells, over 80 percent were associated with product design!"

"Wow, that's a big number," added Brad.

"That's what we thought too," concurred Ken. "And as you know, Brad, the majority of a product's cost is locked in during the design phase."

"So here's where we were," he continued. "We were losing market share. Our customers were telling us our products were costing too much and took too long to develop. We had made some big gains by applying lean concepts in the manufacturing arena, but even this was somewhat tempered by the quality issues we were fighting in the cells. And the data indicated that the quality problems had their roots in the product design. So can you guess what we did next?"

"Go on," urged Brad.

"We saw a major opportunity in applying the lean concepts we had used in manufacturing to our product development process. We believed we could realize similar benefits in terms of eliminating waste, reducing cycle time and cost, and at the same time addressing the quality issues we were fighting in the cells."

"Interesting idea," said Brad. "I have to admit that up until now my understanding of lean principles has been limited to the manufacturing arena. I never gave much thought about applying lean to other areas like product development."

"Based on our success with product development, we've also started to apply these concepts to other business processes as well," declared Ken.

"I'm intrigued," commented Brad, as he paused for a moment to ponder what he'd just heard. "You've mentioned the concept of eliminating waste a couple of times," he continued. "How did you accomplish that?"

"When I talk about eliminating waste," replied Ken, "I'm really talking about activities that don't add any value in the eyes of the customer. In applying lean concepts, a major objective is to identify value-added and non-value-added activities. But in terms of value, it's really with respect to the customer."

"Okay then, so with respect to the customer, what does 'value' really mean?" asked Brad.

"Three conditions must be met for an activity to be truly considered value-added," replied Ken. "The first condition is that the customer must be willing to pay for the activity. In terms of value, this is pretty straightforward. If the customer perceives something is important and is willing to pay for it, in their eyes it is something of value. The second condition is that the activity must in some way alter or change the product. For example, consider the movement of a part from one machine to another, a work order form being routed from one department to the next, storing parts, or any inspection operation. None of these activities change the product in any way, so they are all considered non-value-added activities. And finally, the third condition is that the activity must be done right the first time. If the activity is not performed correctly, the customer certainly will not be willing to pay for it and additional time and effort will be needed in order to replace or correct the product.

"So there you go, Brad," continued Ken. "Value is really based on three conditions. And remember, all three must be satisfied."

"Okay," responded Brad. "I understand what you mean about value-added. So obviously then, in terms of eliminating waste, the goal is to eliminate as many of the non-value-added activities as you can."

"That's right, Brad," replied Ken. "In terms of lean concepts, waste itself can be grouped in any one of seven different categories. These categories are defects, overproduction, inventory, motion, processing, transportation, and waiting. So with regard to eliminating waste, the goal is to attack activities representing these seven categories."

"But in terms of evaluating a process, how do you decide where to begin to eliminate waste?" asked Brad.

"Well, you're on the right track when you refer to a process," suggested Ken. "But it's a little more involved than that. It really involves looking at the entire value stream of a product."

"What's the difference?" asked Brad.

"Typically, when a process is evaluated, the focus is on only the specific activities that do something to the product—in other words, the value-added activities. In contrast, a value stream is the sequence or "flow" of all of the value-added *and* non-value-added activities associated with producing the product. In addition, analysis of a value stream will include the time necessary to complete each specific activity—queue time—which represents the 'waiting time' for the product between each activity, and an assessment of the work-in-process or WIP. Once this information is gathered, it is documented on a map. Appropriately enough, a map of this kind is called a value stream map."

"What you've described is very interesting," responded Brad. "With the information that you've talked about, I can see how the map you've described would provide a comprehensive look at all of the activities that are necessary to support the creation of a product.

"Now I understand how you go about eliminating waste!" he continued. "You identify value-added and non-value-added activities and use a tool like a value stream map to help identify areas of opportunity for improvement."

"Right again, Brad," replied Ken. "As I mentioned earlier, eliminating waste is a key objective in utilizing lean concepts. And looking for waste by examining the entire value stream is a very effective way to make significant improvement."

"I see what you're saying. But I've been on some process improvement teams that have made some really big gains, too," countered Brad.

"I'm sure you have," replied Ken. "Let me clarify what I mean with regard to a value stream and show you why it's so important. At this point, Ken walked over to the white board in the conference room and proceeded to draw the sketch shown in Figure 4.1.

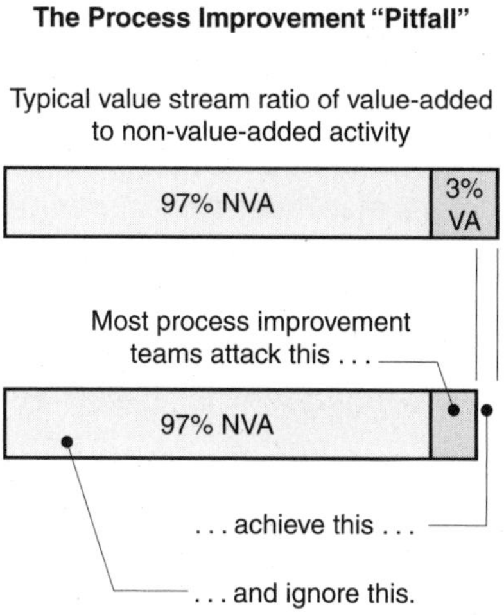

The Process Improvement "Pitfall"

Typical value stream ratio of value-added
to non-value-added activity

97% NVA	3% VA

Most process improvement
teams attack this . . .

97% NVA	

. . . achieve this . . .

. . . and ignore this.

Figure 4.1   Characteristics of process improvement.

"I like to refer to this as the process improvement pitfall," continued Ken. "If you look at a typical value stream, nearly 97 percent of the total time is associated with non-value-added activities—and only 3 percent is associated with adding value for the customer. And this is where the pitfall lies. As I mentioned earlier, evaluation of a process will typically focus on the activities where something is 'being done' to the product—and virtually ignore the non-value-added activities like transportation, queue time, and storage that impact the entire value stream. Consequently, most process improvement teams tend to focus on a very small portion of the value stream and miss the larger opportunity to make significant improvement."

"Very interesting," declared Brad. "So looking at the business from the perspective of the value stream is the key."

"That's right," said Ken. "Within businesses, there are many value streams. In manufacturing, for example, the value stream could be the production flow from the receipt of raw material to the completion of the finished product ready to be shipped to the customer. Or, in the case of product development, the value stream could be the information flow from the receipt of technical requirements from the customer to the completion of blueprints by the engineering department."

"Okay," said Brad. "That brings up an interesting question. How did you use a value stream map in applying lean concepts to your product development process?"

"The value stream map was used in conjunction with conducting a *lean baseline event* for evaluating our product development process," commented Ken.

"A lean baseline event?" asked Brad. "What's that?"

"It's essentially a comprehensive self-assessment of the process you're going to improve. As I mentioned earlier, we already knew the key issues we needed to improve for our product development process in terms of excessive cycle time and high cost. But what we didn't know were the underlying *causes* of our problems. The objectives of the baseline event are to identify where the problems exist, shape a vision for the future, determine where to start and what to do, and obtain management commitment to proceed with an improvement plan. The value stream map was one of the tools we used to help meet the baseline objectives."

"Sounds *very* involved," interjected Brad.

"It can be," added Ken. "A successful baseline event requires participation from all the key players involved in the process. In general, it takes at least a few days, preferably no longer than a week. It also requires some prep work to be done before the actual event begins. From our experience, the baseline event lays the foundation for the follow-on activities. The better the baseline, the better the chances of success and real improvement."

"That makes sense," added Brad. "Like just about everything, to get value out of something you need to put value in."

"Very true, Brad. I couldn't have said it better myself," replied Ken.

"Okay, so what did you learn from the baseline event for your product development process?" asked Brad.

"Well, let me answer that question by first giving you a little more background about Donetics," replied Ken. "As you know, we have basically three product lines: motors and power generation products, engines, and pump systems. The technology we use in our products is pretty stable. Heck, we still ship some products that we designed over 15 years ago! Through a legacy of being in business for 25 years, we now have an extensive product portfolio consisting of many spin-offs of the same basic products.

"In terms of what the baseline event told us, it gave us better insight into our problems and the causes behind them," continued Ken. "For example, here's how our product development process worked using our traditional approach: A customer would come knocking on Donetics's door needing a product. Based on the requirements provided by the customer, we would attempt to use one of our existing products that would come close to matching the customer's needs. You see, since the technology was relatively stable, we were smart enough to recognize that if we could find an existing product that came close to matching the customer's needs, we could potentially reduce design time. The problem was that it was nearly impossible to find an existing product that would be a good match. Success in finding something was based solely on the knowledge and experience of the engineers working the new project."

"So what caused you to get into this position?" asked Brad.

"We had no mechanisms or tools in place to feed information back to engineers," replied Ken. "When an engineering team completed a project, the team would disband and the individuals would be assigned to their next job. There was no feedback to tell the engineering team if they had just created a good design or a bad design. No information to tell if the product worked well or not in the field. Once a project was completed, it fell into a black hole. So understanding this, it's no wonder why we couldn't find a product that matched a customer's requirements. Consequently, our entire engineering organization worked under the premise that it was easier to design a new part than find an existing one! We reinvented the wheel for every product we designed. Every design was a custom design that cost too much and took too long to develop."

"Very interesting," responded Brad. "Did you learn anything else?"

"A couple more key things," added Ken. "As part of the baseline, we reviewed four key projects we recently worked on. What we found out is that we were not very disciplined in following our existing product development process. Compounding that, we did not do a good job of managing our resources. We were very diligent in trying to win new business, but not good at managing our resources to complete the work we were committed to do. As a result, many of our engineers were juggling multiple jobs. The data showed an average of four jobs per engineer. This concept is known as multitasking. Multitasking leads to the creation of bottlenecks that impede the movement of work quickly through the value stream. On the human side, multitasking leads to inefficiency and a higher incidence of mistakes."

"Wow, it sounds like you got to the root of the problem," added Brad. "You obviously put the necessary effort into the baseline to understand the issues. But you also said another objective of the baseline was to shape a vision and determine what to do."

"Very good. You remembered!" kidded Ken. "Seriously though, Brad, you're exactly right. But before I explain to you what we did, let me tell you about some additional lean concepts that we relied on to guide our thinking.

"Based on our earlier discussion, Brad, you're now familiar with concepts of specifying value in the eyes of the customer, eliminating waste, the value stream, and the concept of 'flow.' But when we're dealing with product development, these concepts hold true but are supplemented with some additional lean principles. First, work on what's important.[1] This means picking the right projects with high value for the business that align with the organization's core competencies. Second, concentrate the work.[2] This means ramping up the engineering team as quickly as possible with capable and required resources. In addition, facilitate communication by moving individuals into a shared work area or through the use of teleconferencing and computer hookups. And third, leverage knowledge.[3] This means using appropriate levels of expertise, learning as much as you can, and capturing the knowledge you have."

"Okay," replied Brad. "So you took these principles and concepts and came up with a plan. Right?"

"Exactly," declared Ken. "For us, the third principle I just described was critical. The one about leveraging knowledge. Remember the problem of finding an existing product design we could use for a new customer application?" Brad nodded.

ENDNOTES

1. Reprinted with permission from Kevin Colcord. *Lean Product Development Presentation* (Lean Alliance, version 1.0, dated 2/1/99): 5.
2. Ibid.
3. Ibid.

5

Product Development Approaches

"Here's what we came up with in terms of a plan," replied Ken. At this point, Ken walked over to the whiteboard again and proceeded to draw the sketch shown in Figure 5.1.

"This sketch represents the cornerstone of our new product development approach," he continued. "As you can see, development cycle time increases as you proceed along the horizontal axis from left to right. You can also equate this to product cost and technical risk. Along the vertical axis is reuse, which

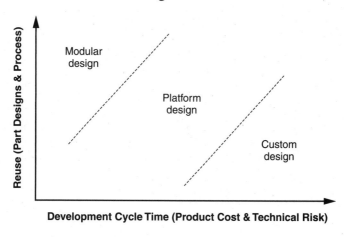

Figure 5.1 Approaches to product development.

relates to part designs and discipline in following the product development process. The level increases as you move from the bottom to the top. Here's the link to the third principle I mentioned earlier about leveraging knowledge and why it was so critical to us. Within the body of the chart are three strategies for product design that cover the spectrum of development cycle time and reuse. Prior to our lean effort, Donetics operated exclusively in the custom design region where product cost and cycle times were high. You said it yourself, Brad. And the level of reuse was extremely low. Through our lean effort, we have developed two additional strategies for product development."

"So, Ken, if I understand what you're saying, you have three strategies for product development. But why didn't you eliminate the custom design approach? After all, isn't that what got you into trouble in the first place?" asked Brad.

"Not really," responded Ken. "A custom design in not necessarily a bad thing. It's all about leverage."

"I know," interjected Brad. "Your lean principle of leveraging knowledge, right?"

"Well, not exactly," said Ken. "I'm talking about a slightly different kind of leverage here."

"Huh?"

"I'm talking about leverage with the customer," said Ken.

"I don't get it," confessed Brad.

"Let me explain," continued Ken, referring once again to the chart. "As I mentioned earlier, Donetics operated entirely in the lower right region of the chart; the custom design region where costs are high and cycle times are long. But now, depending on which product development approach we employ, we have begun to migrate toward the upper left region of the chart where cycle times are shorter, costs are lower, and reuse levels and process discipline are high.

"So let's go back to the example I used earlier about a customer knocking on our door needing a new product. Now, based on the customer's requirements and the level of reuse, Donetics can respond to the customer and say, for example,

'Customer A, here is a product that we have that will meet your needs and we can offer it to you for X price and provide it to you in Y time frame.' Or we could say, 'Customer A, here is a product that comes *close* to meeting your needs and if you can modify your requirement to $Z,$ we can offer it to you for X price and provide it to you in Y time frame.' If the customer is not willing to modify the requirement, that's okay too. But it might result in a higher cost and an increase in cycle time in order to accommodate the requirement. The point here is that through our product development strategies, we now have leverage with the customer in terms of providing them options and choices that they never had before. If the customer wants a total custom design, a totally reused design, or something in between, Donetics is in a position to provide it for them.

"So that's why a custom design is not necessarily a bad thing. After giving the customer a choice, if they decide they need a special product, can live with the schedule and are willing to pay for it, we'll give it to them."

"Okay," responded Brad. "I see what you mean about leverage with the customer. From my own perspective, this is exactly what we're looking for from our suppliers. With this approach, you would be informing us of the trade-offs, and we would decide what's most important."

"Exactly!" proclaimed Ken.

"So now tell me *how* you accomplished this. Let's hear about the modular design and platform design approaches," queried Brad.

6

Modular Design

"**L**et's start with the modular design approach," replied Ken. "The first thing to tell you is that the term 'modular design' is really derived from the word 'module,' or 'subassembly.' So in other words, the modular design strategy is essentially an approach based on reusing modules, or subassemblies.

"Consider an automobile, for example. It is a product representing a modular design approach. An automobile can be divided into various subassemblies such as the engine, frame assembly, steering column assembly, passenger seat assembly, dashboard assembly, and so on. There are many other examples of products with modular characteristics, such as personal computers, kitchen appliances, power tools, bicycles, and even the International Space Station. It was transported and assembled in space using a modular approach."

"Okay," said Brad. "I understand conceptually how the modular design approach works. But what if you can't modularize the whole product?"

"Then do the next best thing. Reuse an individual part. That's exactly what we did in applying the modular concept in our engine product line. The major parts of a typical engine consist of a carburetor, a flywheel subassembly, a pull-cord subassembly, and a main engine block and piston subassembly.

But the plate cover component that mates with the engine block subassembly was not a logical fit in terms of being a component of the module, so we attempted to reuse an existing part design from the entire family of plate covers that we've created over time."

"So what you're saying," added Brad, "is that the modular design strategy for a product can really be geared toward reusing a combination of modules and individual parts."

"That's right," said Ken. "I'd say that's probably the case for most products. For our gas-powered engine, we analyzed the product and determined the combination of modules and individual parts that we needed."

"How did you do that?" asked Brad. "And what did you mean when you said the cover was not a logical fit for a module?"

"Two very good questions," replied Ken. "Let me explain. We start with a tool called a *product breakdown structure.*"

"A product breakdown structure?" repeated Brad.

"Yes," continued Ken. "It's essentially a tree diagram that starts at the finished product level and breaks down the product into pieces. Let's go back to the automobile example I used earlier and see how we could apply a product breakdown structure to this product." At this point, Ken once again walked over to the white board and proceeded to draw the sketch shown in Figure 6.1.

"This is by no means a complete product breakdown structure for an automobile," continued Ken. "But it does hopefully convey the concept of how it works. Starting at the product level, an automobile is divided into three pieces at the major assembly level. In practice, each major assembly would be further subdivided, but for our purposes we'll just focus on one. Next, the body is then broken down into smaller pieces, represented by the module level. Finally, the modules themselves can be broken down further into the various individual parts."

"I think I get it," declared Brad. "You start at the top with the product, and basically keep breaking it down into smaller pieces."

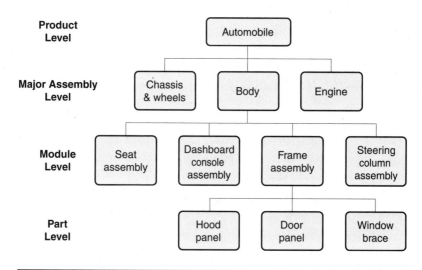

Figure 6.1 Product breakdown structure example.

"That's right," replied Ken. "You can think of the product breakdown structure as the road map to identify reuse opportunities. The more complex the product is, the more complex the product breakdown structure will be."

"I see your point, Ken," interjected Brad. "The product breakdown structure could become pretty complex. But if I understand correctly, you don't have to identify *every* component down to the part level. Right?"

"That's correct, Brad," replied Ken. "If you're able to reuse a module, there's no benefit to breaking down the product beyond that level. The key point to remember is that the purpose of the product breakdown structure is to identify reuse opportunities. Once you've done that, there's no point to going any further."

"Okay," said Brad. "But that brings me back to my second question, which you haven't answered yet. How do you determine which parts to include in the module? You said the plate cover wasn't a logical fit in a module, remember?"

"I was coming to that," replied Ken. "I think the best way for me to answer that question is to explain the way we used to design our engines prior to adopting the modular design strategy. As you know, our typical engine consists of approximately 100 individual parts; roughly 60 custom parts and 40 commodity parts. Commodity parts are parts like nuts, bolts, pins, clips, and so on. When the engineering group would initiate a new product design, the assembly drawing for the product would list all 100 parts. Then, when it was time to assemble the product, all 100 parts would be requisitioned by the mechanic to assemble the product."

"That makes sense," said Brad. "But I don't see how this relates to my question."

"Think about the mechanic who now has to assemble the product," offered Ken. "How do you think he would assemble the product? How do you think he would deal with 100 individual parts?"

"I don't know," speculated Brad. "He would just start putting it together."

"But *how*?" repeated Ken.

"I don't get it," responded Brad, confused.

"It turns out that the mechanic was assembling the product in a modular fashion!" declared Ken. "He would create subassemblies for the flywheel, pull-cord, carburetor, and so on, and then put them all together."

"Wow, that's really interesting," replied Brad.

"Yeah, we thought so too," added Ken. "After we reviewed the assembly build work instructions that the mechanic uses, we discovered that the Operations people have been doing this for years. The point here is that in some cases the parts that define a module can be rather obvious; such as in the case of solenoids that we purchase for our motors, for example, that are fully self-contained units that are bolted onto our products. But for other cases where it is not obvious, the Operations people and the assembly build work instructions for the product are excellent sources to help define modules. In the case of the plate cover, the work instructions indicated that based on the assembly sequence required for the product, the cover needed to be installed at the very end after the other subassemblies were put together."

"Okay, now I understand," responded Brad. "I see what you mean about the cover not being a logical fit. In this case, the assembly sequence influenced the definition of the module."

"I think you've got it, Brad," replied Ken. "In the case of our gas-powered engines, you could say that through modular design, Engineering has adopted a philosophy of developing the product in a way that mirrors how Operations will assemble the product. Through the modular design effort, a key takeaway that our engineering people have learned is that if you can't assemble it, you shouldn't design it."

"That's really insightful," responded Brad. "What better way to help bridge the gap between Engineering and Operations. At Terra Solutions we're always trying to address that issue."

"So," continued Brad, "I understand what a product breakdown structure is and how to use it. But once you've decided what the reuse opportunity is, how do you know which specific part designs to reuse?"

"Another excellent question, Brad," commented Ken. "That brings us up to the next step; the utilization of part families."

"The utilization of part families!" exclaimed Brad. "That sounds like a subtitle to a science fiction movie."

"Oh brother!" said Ken with a laugh.

"Sorry. I couldn't resist," chuckled Brad.

"That's okay. That's okay. You'll see," said Ken. "You won't be making jokes about part families once you understand how important they are."

"Please go on."

"Your question is right on, Brad. In order to reuse a part design, you first need to know what you've got. Pretty logical, huh?" suggested Ken.

"I'm with you so far," replied Brad.

"Let's go back once more to the plate cover. We said earlier that we would reuse an existing part design, right? But in order to do that, we first needed to know how many covers we could choose from. In other words, we needed to know the entire family of plate cover parts that we had at our disposal to support our reuse strategy."

"Didn't you already have that information?" asked Brad.

"In the case of the plate covers, not really," responded Ken. "Remember our old way of operating? Our designs going into a black hole? So we had to spend some time identifying the parts that were represented in the family. One way that was pretty successful was to use our enterprise resource planning (ERP) system and perform nomenclature searches to query the system for the parts we were looking for. There are a couple of other ways to do it. But it really depends on how much knowledge you have about the part family."

"So is that it?" asked Brad.

"Not hardly," replied Ken. "At this point, we simply knew the part numbers that were represented by the family. But nothing more. The fundamental question still remained of deciding what to reuse. To accomplish this, it was necessary to catalog information about the parts so we could decide which part designs were best to reuse."

"Catalog information about the parts?" asked Brad.

"Yeah," replied Ken. "We cataloged the parts based on their attributes. An attribute is a piece of information or characteristic that describes the part.

"The attributes are identified at the module and part family levels. In the case of the plate cover part family, we cataloged 17 attributes such as the material, cover type, port style and location, size dimensions, interface dimensions for mating parts, and others. Once the attributes were identified, the next task was to review the individual part drawings to extract the data. We built simple spreadsheets to capture and catalog the attribute data for all of the parts in the family."

"I see," said Brad. "You now had information about the parts to help you decide which ones to reuse."

"Exactly," confirmed Ken.

"Did you catalog every piece of data on the engineering drawings that describe the parts?" asked Brad.

"No, not quite," replied Ken. "It would become pretty overwhelming to catalog every attribute for every part in the family. But there's really a fine line in deciding how many attributes to catalog. You really want to capture enough attributes so there's enough detail in the data for a user to find a few key candidates with reuse potential, and not so few so that the data is vague and there are too many parts to consider."

"So now you had the data to describe the parts in the family," commented Brad. "At this point you can select parts to reuse, right?"

"Well, yes and no," waffled Ken.

"Huh?"

"Well, yes from the standpoint that you now have enough data to enable you to select a part design," continued Ken. "But no from the perspective of reuse. Consider these questions. What if I reuse a part design with a high scrap rate? Or one with exceptionally high cost? Or one that doesn't function properly?"

"I see your point," responded Brad. "Some parts you may *not* want to reuse."

"That's right, Brad."

"So what do you do?" asked Brad.

"The last step," continued Ken. "The selection of preferred parts."

"Preferred parts?" repeated Brad.

"Yes," said Ken. "The term 'preferred part' is nothing more than a label that we've assigned to certain part designs. It designates the part designs that we want to promote for reuse. Let me throw some numbers at you. In the case of the plate cover part family, we cataloged attribute data for 126 part designs. In other words, we were able to identify that, over time, we've created 126 different plate cover parts. Of those 126, we identified 12 as preferred parts."

"How did you select the 12 parts?" asked Brad.

"Our engineering experts reviewed data on all of the parts in the family and selected the preferred ones. They reviewed not only the cataloged attribute data, but also cost data, manufacturing data, quality data and, if available, performance data.

"The criteria for selecting the preferred parts depends on the part family. Some of the criteria are generic to all part families, such as cost, scrap rates, and quality levels. But other criteria are specifically related to the part family, such as the attribute data."

"Okay," said Brad. "That makes sense. So let me make sure I understand what you've told me. You've outlined three steps that support your reuse strategy. Do you mind if I use your white board?"

"By all means," responded Ken, while gesturing to him to approach the board. Brad proceeded to draw the sketch shown in Figure 6.2.

"So once the reuse opportunity is identified from the product breakdown structure, this process kicks in," commented Brad, referring to his sketch.

"That's right, Brad," responded Ken. "We've replicated the process you've drawn there for about 30 different part families in the engine product line. I like to refer to it as the reuse infrastructure."

"A reuse infrastructure. I kind of like that," said Brad.

"The reuse infrastructure is really the enabler to make the modular design approach work," added Ken.

"So the plan is to use the preferred parts as much as you can in your product designs, right?" asked Brad.

"That's the goal," continued Ken. "We want to reduce variation in our product designs by leveraging our existing product

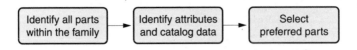

Figure 6.2 Process for developing preferred parts.

portfolio and reusing as much as we can. Within our engine product line, our strategy has been to create new versions of the same basic product."

"And the modular design approach gets you there!" interjected Brad.

"Exactly," replied Ken. "You can think of the modular design approach as representing a hierarchy of reuse. The goal is to reuse modules and preferred parts. If you can't, then the next best thing is to reuse an existing non-preferred part design. It's still better than making a new part. Finally, if all else fails and there are no other options, then create a new part. Using the modular approach, we've started to make some quantum gains in terms of reducing product development cycle time and cost in our engine product line."

"Very impressive! Very impressive, indeed!" declared Brad. "Now I understand how you were able to generate a proposal for a new Atlas engine in an hour and a half. You applied the concept of reuse and leveraged your existing product portfolio to create a new one. The modular design concept works!

"But you also outlined another strategy for product development. You referred to it as the platform design approach. Can you give me a little insight into what this is and how it differs from the modular design approach?"

"Sure," replied Ken. "By the way, can I offer you anything else to drink?"

"No thanks, Ken," responded Brad. "Actually, I'm still working on my coffee."

"Okay. I just wanted to make sure I was being a good host," cajoled Ken.

"You always are," smirked Brad. "In all honesty, I'm so intrigued in what you're telling me, I don't even want to take a break."

"Fair enough," replied Ken.

7

Platform Design

"The reason for different product development strategies is borne out of the inherent differences in the products they support," stated Ken. "Let me explain.

"As you now know, the modular design strategy is centered around the creation of modules or subassemblies; the logical groupings of parts like flywheels, carburetors, and so on, that perform specific functions. In many cases, these subassemblies can be easily interchanged with others to accommodate the requirements of different products. For example, if the same engine product is used on different cutting deck and handle designs for a lawn mower, we can generally use a specific pull-cord module to accommodate differences in handle and deck spacing. Basically, a module can be used in a plug-and-play mode.

"Now, let's contrast this approach with a product supported by the platform design strategy. With this type of product, there is a higher degree of dependency between the individual components. All of the parts must work together to perform the product's primary function. Consequently, products of this nature are not conducive to the plug-and-play approach with modules. A good example of a product fitting this strategy would be a commercial jet engine. In this case, the jet engine is designed to meet a certain thrust requirement. The individual parts all work in tandem and are sized to meet the requirement. Generally, it's not possible to replace or resize one or two parts to change the product's overall performance. It's kind of like a domino effect. If you change one part, it affects another, then another, and so on. In other words, you can think of the product as representing a platform, or baseline design. If you need a different thrust requirement, you typically need an entirely new product. It's as if the entire engine design would need to be 'scaled' up or down in order to meet the different requirement."

"Okay, based on your explanation, I understand the fundamental differences in the products supported by the different strategies," commented Brad. "So what do you do differently with the platform design approach?"

"Essentially, the overall goals are the same in terms of reducing product cycle time and cost," replied Ken. "But the approach is different. Here, as opposed to reusing existing modules and parts, we're creating a new product based on an existing design; the platform design. Also, because we're making a new design, a key goal of the platform design approach is to manage the technical risk in creating the new product. As you know, it's critically important that the new product work as it's intended the first time out in order to avoid a subsequent redesign. This is important not only from a customer satisfaction perspective, but also from a business perspective."

"That's absolutely correct," said Brad. "So how do you manage the technical risk?"

"There are three tools that we use to help manage the risk," replied Ken. "The first one is called a *technical requirements flow-down matrix,* the second is a *product experience domain,* and the third is a *component design compliance matrix.* Let's take a closer look at each one.

"The technical requirements flow-down matrix provides a consistent way to evaluate the technical requirements for a new product. By using the matrix, we have instilled discipline in the evaluation process, standardized the approach, and when referenced against a baseline product, have a clear understanding of the areas of non-compliance. The matrix itself is nothing more than a simple spreadsheet. Here are the key elements of the matrix." Ken approached the white board and proceeded to draw the sketch shown in Figure 7.1.

"Each technical requirement is denoted on the matrix and measured against the characteristics of a platform product design," continued Ken. "In addition, after assessing the requirement against the baseline, we make a recommendation on how to address the requirement based on the priority and the parts that are impacted by the requirement."

"I see," replied Brad. "It looks like a pretty rigorous process. And it also lays the foundation for future activity, right?"

"That's exactly right, Brad," said Ken. "With the completed matrix, we know right where the gaps exist and can plan our efforts to eliminate them."

"Okay," replied Brad. "What about the other tools you mentioned. Wasn't the second one called the experienced compliance domain?"

"Close," chuckled Ken. "It's called the product experience domain."

"Sorry," replied Brad. "It's hard to keep up with all of these fancy names you keep throwing around."

"You're right, Brad," responded Ken. "It can be a little confusing. After explaining these two tools, I won't use any more fancy names."

"Fair enough," said Brad. "Please go on."

Technical requirement description	Document reference	Baseline product assessment	Donetics recommendation	Priority	Affected part

Figure 7.1 Technical requirements flow-down matrix example.

"The product experience domain is a tool that can take on a couple of different forms. It could be in the form of cataloged data, similar to the modular design approach; a data table; or a graphical display. In any case, the product experience domain is a tool that really represents design variables that are essential to a product's performance, reliability, and quality. In other words, it is the first step in characterizing products and subsystems, and helps in identifying risk by denoting areas where experience exists. Here's an example of one."

Ken drew another sketch on the white board (see Figure 7.2).

"Let's say we're evaluating performance parameters such as engine speed versus vibration," continued Ken, referring to the sketch. "The graph shows the performance of six actual products against these parameters, represented by products A through F. Based on the scatter of the existing products on the graph, two distinct groups represented by the circles are formed.

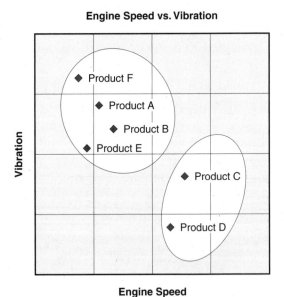

Figure 7.2 Product experience domain example.

These circles represent the regions or areas of experience based on the performance of the existing products.

"So now let's say we're creating a new product. The performance of the new product for engine speed versus vibration would be derived and referenced against this product experience domain. If the data point for the new product falls within one of the two circled regions, then the new product's performance is within the range of our experience and existing product portfolio in terms of this parameter. There would be a high degree of certainty in terms of the product design and its performance with regard to this parameter. However, if the data point falls outside of the two circled regions, then the new product's performance is beyond the current experience level. This would imply that the new design imposes some risk with regard to this performance parameter. The farther away the new product's data point is from the circled regions, the higher the degree of risk. At this point, additional work would need to be done to either modify the product design and mitigate the risk or evaluate the potential impact of the risk from a business and engineering perspective."

"Very interesting," replied Brad. "With my engineering background, I really can appreciate the analytical approach you've taken to understanding the levels of risk."

"I agree," added Ken. "It's a methodical approach that quantifies the risk. The numbers speak for themselves.

"To this point, we have put together a comprehensive library of product experience domains, but there are still more that we need to create," he said. "The goal is to address all of the key design and performance parameters that support products in our power generation product line."

"I see," commented Brad. "It sounds like you're putting considerable effort into creating these product experience domains."

"It's really an investment," replied Ken. "By creating the product experience domains, we've developed a better understanding about the capabilities of our own products. The more we know about our products, the better job we will do in the future in creating new ones—and have them work correctly the first time!"

"That makes an awful lot of sense," interjected Brad.

"In terms of the investment, if we avoid only one product redesign, it will more than pay for the total effort in creating the product experience domains," said Ken. "And for us, it already has.

"And one more thing, Brad. If you think about it, the product experience domains really represent another example of building the reuse infrastructure we talked about earlier. Remember the lean principle about leveraging knowledge?"

"That's right!" exclaimed Brad. "I didn't think about it that way until you just mentioned it, but you're right!

"Okay, I remember there's one more tool that you're going to tell me about for the platform strategy, but I'm not going to guess the name of this one!" confessed Brad.

"I understand. A little gun-shy after botching the last one?" joked Ken.

"Well, let's just call me a patient listener," replied Brad.

"Okay, if you say so," said Ken with a smile. "The last tool is called a *component design compliance matrix.* Like the technical requirements flow-down matrix, this tool is arranged in a spreadsheet format. Its primary function is to assist in developing actions when component designs don't meet the minimum requirements. Here are the key elements of a component design compliance matrix."

Once again, Ken approached the whiteboard and drew the sketch shown in Figure 7.3.

Design requirement	Design criteria	Validation methodology	Rating to accepted standard	Experience	Proposed mitigation of noncompliance

Figure 7.3   Component design compliance matrix example.

"As you can see based on the column headings," continued Ken, "the component design compliance matrix is another example of using a tool to provide a measure of consistency in our product development process. The design requirements for a specific component are listed in the matrix. In addition, information is documented that assesses our ability to meet and verify the requirement. Finally, mitigation plans are noted to address areas of noncompliance. Like product experience domains, we are currently building a library of component design compliance matrices. A separate matrix will exist for each key component for products within our power generation product line."

"This is another good example of using a tool to instill discipline in your process," commented Brad.

"Very insightful," responded Ken.

"And based on your explanation, I can also see how the three tools you described for the platform strategy can work together," continued Brad. "The technical requirements flowdown matrix provides consistency in evaluating customer needs and desires. The product experience domains allow you to leverage the knowledge of your existing products and identify areas of risk for new product designs. And the component design compliance matrix helps to insure you design new components that meet the design requirements."

"Wow, you got it!" declared Ken.

"And did you notice I got the names of the tools right?" cajoled Brad.

"Yes, you did!" joked Ken.

"Seriously though," said Brad. "What you've described to me are obviously two very effective strategies. And what's more, they are based on some pretty basic ideas."

"That's right, Brad," replied Ken. "Regardless of which strategy that's used, we now have a measure of consistency and discipline that was previously lacking in our product development process. And it was accomplished by following some basic lean principles—like leveraging knowledge."

8

Data Management

"But that brings up another interesting question," interjected Brad. "It's quite obvious now, after understanding the modular design and platform design approaches, that there are a lot of data needed to support the product development process—such as attribute data for part families, preferred parts, product experience domains, and so on. How do you manage all of that data?"

"Good question," replied Ken. "And you're right, there are lots of data. Quite simply, we built a simple database to manage the information. We even gave it a name. We call it the *product development tool.*

"After we started gathering some of the data," continued Ken, "we realized that in order to make the new product development approaches truly effective, we needed to provide the users, our engineers, with the information they needed, when they needed it. In other words, the database provides point-of-use information to the individuals who need it. Here are the key pieces of information that are represented in the product development tool." Ken drew a sketch on the whiteboard (see Figure 8.1).

"Based on our discussion," continued Ken, "you obviously recognize some of the tools and data pieces. But a key thing that we've done to make the tool really effective is to link the

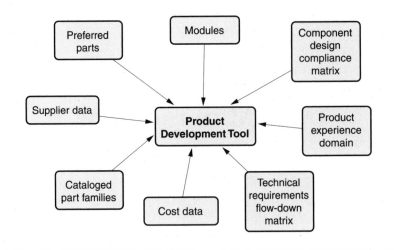

Figure 8.1   Data elements of a product development tool.

product development data with enterprise resource planning, ERP, data. By doing this, our engineers have access to cost data, part usage requirements, part inventory levels, supplier identification, and other purchasing information. From a user's perspective, this data provides a comprehensive picture that enables them to make the right decisions in support of the reuse philosophy. In that respect, you can really think of the database as being an extension of the reuse infrastructure we talked about earlier."

"I see," replied Brad. "Interesting approach to address the data management issue. How did you go about creating the database?"

"It's really been an evolutionary process," responded Ken. "When we first started our product development effort, we had no idea what role a database would play and certainly no idea what one would look like. But as the overall effort progressed and we started capturing data to which we knew we wanted future access, the vision became much clearer. For example, let's take a look at the cataloged data for the various part families we discussed earlier for the modular design approach. For this feature in the product development tool, we developed a two-step process for providing the data. The first step, as I mentioned earlier, was to build simple spreadsheets to capture the data. Here's what a typical spreadsheet looked like." Ken drew another sketch on the whiteboard (see Figure 8.2).

"The spreadsheet is structured with the attributes as the column headings and the part numbers designated in the rows," continued Ken. "Within the body of the spreadsheet is the cataloged data for each part number. The size of the spreadsheet is dependent upon the number of attributes and the quantity of part numbers within the part family."

"It sounds like a pretty straightforward approach," commented Brad. "So what's the second step?"

"Well," responded Ken, "capturing the cataloged data was a major accomplishment. But we then realized that having the data in spreadsheet form was not a very user-friendly way to find information. Some of the spreadsheets became quite large. So the second step was to create a database 'front end' that would enable a user to quickly navigate within the part family data and extract the key information they were looking for. To further explain what I mean, let's refer once again to the plate cover part family.

"As we discussed earlier, the cataloged data for the plate cover family contains 17 attributes supporting 126 parts. However, as a first step in finding part designs with reuse potential, it's really not necessary to evaluate *all* 17 attributes.

Part numbers	Attribute 1	Attribute 2	Attribute 3	Attribute 4	Attribute 5	Attribute 6
Part number 1						
Part number 2						
Part number 3			Cataloged			
Part number 4			Data			
Part number 5						

Figure 8.2 Spreadsheet structure for cataloging part attribute data.

In reality, only a subset of the 17 attributes represents critical, or what I call 'predominant' information for searching for parts within the family. The balance of attributes provides additional information for plate cover parts to further discriminate parts within the family. The database front end is essentially a search screen that allows a user to select from among the predominant attributes. Obviously, the more attributes that are selected by the user, the more focused the database search will be. Once the user has completed the attribute selection, the information is submitted to the database. The database responds with a printed report listing the part numbers that meet the search criteria. In addition, the printout includes all of the cataloged data for each identified part as well as any available cost and supplier data."

"Interesting," replied Brad. "I see what you mean about it being an evolutionary approach."

"It really is," confirmed Ken. "We've replicated the two-step approach I described for all of the other part families for which we've cataloged data. In addition, with the inclusion of the other data elements we've talked about, we've put together a fairly comprehensive database."

"Has the tool met your needs?" queried Brad.

"Very much so," answered Ken. "In some respects the tool is still a work-in-progress. History has shown that many of the users who got a glimpse of the tool and liked it asked for functionality it currently did not provide. In many cases, we added the requested functionality in order to meet their needs. That process is still going on today.

"But there is one pitfall associated with the product development tool. Many people have viewed the tool as the solution to our product development problems. The key point to remember is that the tool is not the solution to the problem, but the enabler to make the process work. The tool supports the new process."

"I think that's an excellent point," stated Brad. "I can relate that to some of my own experiences in the past where we've spent a lot of money in procuring a new tool or a new system, thinking that would be the solution to the problem. But the reality was that it didn't, because we didn't do anything to change the process. Fancy and expensive tools don't fix bad processes!"

"I agree," added Ken. "Sometimes, though, that's a hard lesson to learn."

"So, Ken," said Brad, "I don't mean to put you on the spot, but now that you've explained your new product development process, what has it meant in terms of overall benefit to your business?"

"Well, that brings up another interesting topic," said Ken.

"What do you mean? Are you trying to avoid answering my question?" queried Brad slyly.

"On the contrary," replied Ken. "I'm really trying to answer your question. But in terms of an overall benefit, there's a key piece we haven't even talked about yet.

9

Supply Chain Impact

"Up to this point, we've talked about various product development strategies," said Ken. "And we also talked about the problems we were trying to fix. Remember, you said it yourself Brad: our products took too long to bring to market and cost too much."

Brad nodded in agreement.

"That brings me to my point," he continued. "In order to meet the goals of bringing our products to market more quickly and at a lower price, we realized that we not only needed to *develop* product designs more efficiently, but we also needed to be able to *procure* the hardware more quickly and at a lower cost.

"We manufacture a small percentage of the hardware we use in our products. The rest is procured through our supply base. For many of the electromechanical components we purchase, such as torque motors and solenoids, as well as parts produced from castings, the lead times are often over 30 weeks.

"The product development strategies we've talked about will realize benefits in terms of creating a product design and associated drawings in a significantly shorter time than it used to under the old approach. But they do nothing in terms of getting the hardware in the door that we need to build the product. Based on the current lead times and cost considerations, we came to the conclusion that unless we fundamentally changed the procurement process for our parts, we wouldn't be able to meet our overall goal."

"Wow!" said Brad. "I see your point. What you're describing is the impact of the supply chain in meeting your goal."

"That's right, Brad."

"So what did you do?" he asked.

"Well, to explain what we did, let's go back one more time and use the plate cover part family as an example," replied Ken. "If you remember, we had identified and cataloged through the modular design approach 126 different plate cover parts represented in the family."

"Yes, I remember," replied Brad.

"Well," said Ken, "we decided to take a look at the profile of the suppliers that were manufacturing those 126 parts. And what we found was very interesting. Through our traditional procurement process, we found that 16 different suppliers were being used to manufacture those 126 parts! Here's the distribution of the supplier and the quantity of part numbers that each produced for the family."

Ken drew the sketch shown in Figure 9.1 on the whiteboard.

"As you can see by the distribution in the Pareto chart I've drawn," continued Ken, "we have a few predominant suppliers,

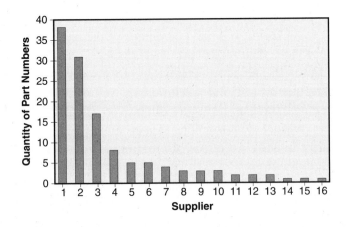

Figure 9.1   Pareto chart for supplier and part number distribution.

and many that produce only a few parts. Of the 16 suppliers, 12 have 5 or less part numbers.

"After reviewing this data, a number of questions come to mind. Do we really need 16 different suppliers producing the same type of part? What about the core competencies of the suppliers and their ability to manufacture this type of part? Are we truly getting competitive pricing from the suppliers that are producing only a few of the part numbers in the family?"

"You bring up some good questions," interjected Brad. "The idea here is that until you looked at the parts on a family basis, you couldn't ask those questions."

"Bingo!" replied Ken. "That's the key point. You see, under the traditional procurement process, when engineering would complete a drawing package, it would be thrown over the wall to the procurement organization, who would source the parts to the suppliers on a part number by part number basis. So, by following this approach for a number of years, it's really not that hard to understand why we were in the position of having 16 suppliers for our plate covers."

"So you saw this as an opportunity to improve on the traditional procurement process, right?" asked Brad.

"That's right," responded Ken. "But actually for a couple of reasons. Our supply base was quite large. We saw an opportunity to improve our efficiency by reducing our overall supply base to a selected number of key suppliers, and by matching those suppliers' manufacturing capability to the part requirements. And the strategy to help us get there was to re-source our parts on a *part family* basis."

"An interesting concept," replied Brad as he thought for a moment. "A part family basis . . . how did you go about doing that? I mean, how did you decide what parts to give to which supplier?"

"Good question," replied Ken. "We used a subgrouping strategy to break the part family into logical pieces as a prelude to the re-source activity."

"You lost me with that one," replied Brad.

"Sorry," said Ken, with a chuckle. "Let me demonstrate this concept with a simple example. Let's say we wanted to do some comparative pricing for automobiles. If we first considered *all* available automobiles, we wouldn't be able to compare prices effectively due to the large variety of vehicle types, model styles, engine sizes, and so on. The point here is that because there are so many characteristics of automobiles to consider, it would be difficult to perform effective price comparisons. But, however, if we use some of the more important characteristics and identify the products accordingly, we could then break down the 'family' of automobiles into pieces, or subgroupings, that make sense for effective price comparisons.

"To illustrate this, I'm going to use a tree diagram once again." Ken approached the white board and drew the diagram shown in Figure 9.2.

"So now let's take this example one step further and say we want to focus on sport utility vehicles. By leveraging what we identify as the important characteristics for this category, such as wheel drive and bed length, we can break sport utility vehicles into even smaller groupings. Then, by identifying the

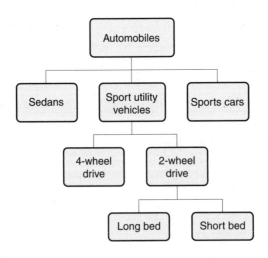

Figure 9.2   Tree diagram creating product subgroupings.

products that fit into that grouping, we can perform effective price comparisons. So, for example, referring to one grouping at the bottom of the tree, we could then perform effective price comparisons for all short bed, two-wheel drive, sport utility vehicles."

"Okay, I understand what you're saying," said Brad. "You divided the product into groups to make the subsequent activity more effective. In your example, you first grouped the products to insure you were comparing apples to apples, in order to make the price comparison more meaningful."

"That's right," confirmed Ken.

"I see a lot of parallels between what you're demonstrating here and the product breakdown structure we talked about earlier," interjected Brad.

"Very true," concurred Ken. "The application of the tool is similar, but the objective is different. With the product breakdown structure, we were identifying reuse opportunities. Here, we're breaking down a part family into pieces to support the re-source activity and to identify the parts."

"Okay. So let me ask a similar question to one that I asked before," said Brad smugly. "How do you identify the variables you use to break down the part family into pieces?"

"The variables are based on the design and manufacturing requirements that are unique to each part family," answered Ken. "Remember what our objectives are for the supply base? Together, the design and manufacturing requirements drive the cost of the part. From a supplier's perspective, this approach of utilizing part families has a significant impact in terms of standardizing work processes, simplifying inspection requirements, reducing setup times, and so on. Leveraged against a family of common parts, these factors provide economies of scale that can significantly reduce part cost."

"Okay, I see what you're saying about the engineering and manufacturing implications for the part family," said Brad. "And the benefits it can provide to a supplier. So have you made significant gains in utilizing this approach?"

"Let's refer again to the plate cover part family," said Ken. "To give you a little more background on this family, essentially all of our plate cover parts fall into one of three different configurations. In addition, plate covers are produced from basically two different materials—material A for high vibration applications and material B for low vibration applications. The different configurations and material of the plate covers are needed to meet certain design requirements, but these variables have manufacturing implications as well. Material A is much more difficult to machine than material B, and the configuration of the part influences the manufacturing process, the machines used to manufacture the parts, and even possibly the tooling. Applying these variables and the subgrouping strategy for the family, here's what we got." Ken drew another sketch on the whiteboard (see Figure 9.3).

"Six subgroups are created based on the combination of configuration and material," continued Ken. "The numbers below the material blocks on the bottom of the tree are the quantities of parts numbers within each subgroup. Following this analysis, the procurement organization was engaged to re-source the subgroups to the key suppliers. But there's a key point to real success in utilizing this strategy. When the parts are re-sourced, they are placed with selected suppliers on a

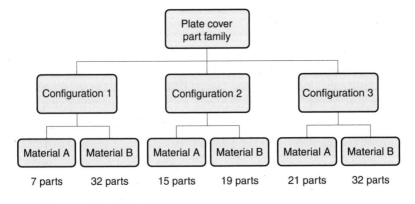

Figure 9.3 Part number impact on family subgroups.

subgroup by subgroup basis. In other words, all of the parts *within* a specific subgroup are placed to only *one* supplier. This approach provides the greatest leverage for the supplier, which, in turn, results in the greatest cost benefits for us. A true partnering relationship!

"In terms of benefits for this family of parts, we reduced the number of suppliers from 16 to two and realized a 28 percent annual cost reduction."

"Wow! Significant savings indeed," declared Brad.

"Very much so," agreed Ken. "Based on the money we spend on procuring our parts, plus the additional savings and overhead costs from managing fewer suppliers, the cost savings is literally in the millions of dollars each year for Donetics."

"Certainly a significant impact to your bottom line," commented Brad. "What you've clearly demonstrated are the downstream benefits to manufacturing and the supply chain resulting from your lean product development activity.

"Okay," continued Brad. "I understand the process you just described for consolidating the supply base for existing parts that were in your system, but what about new parts that are being created by the engineering department? How do you fit this supply base strategy into your product development process?"

"Good question," replied Ken. "The answer is that you want to integrate the supply base strategy as early as possible in the product development process. In other words, you want to engage the selected supplier for the component very early in the product development process and solicit input that could impact the downstream manufacturing of the component.

"As we discussed earlier, the majority of the product cost is locked in early in the design process. But this is also a time when the engineering department has the greatest degree of flexibility with the product design and represents the best opportunity to make significant changes that could influence manufacturing-related issues that the supplier will ultimately have to deal with. As a way to help the engineering department solicit this input, we have embedded the identification of the selected suppliers for the various part families into the product development tool we talked about earlier. So, for example, if a designer was creating a new plate cover component, the individual could access the product development tool and determine very early in the design phase the appropriate supplier who will be manufacturing the component."

"Very interesting," replied Brad. "What you've described really closes the loop by flowing the information from the supply chain back to the engineering department. In a classic sense, it represents a great example of the concept of concurrent engineering."

"That's true, Brad," said Ken. "But there's another benefit for the procurement organization in following this approach. By now having preselected suppliers for the various part families, it has virtually eliminated the process of canvassing the supply base in order to find a supplier for producing a new component. Now, with the new approach, the only remaining activity is to negotiate a price for the new component. And even this is somewhat simplified, because the quoted price for the new component can be leveraged against the other parts in the subgroup produced by the same supplier to insure a measure of consistency. The benefits have been tremendous. This approach has virtually eliminated the need of finding a supplier and eliminated a quoting and bidding process that took an average of five weeks for the procurement organization!"

"That's fantastic," concluded Brad. "It's really interesting to see how the benefits you describe have touched upon the different aspects of the value stream that you talked about earlier."

"Very good point," replied Ken.

10

The Lean and Six Sigma Connection

"**B**ut there's still one thing I'm curious about," continued Brad. "How does Design for Six Sigma, or DFSS, relate to the lean concepts we've been discussing today? I've heard a lot about both topics, but I have to admit I'm somewhat confused about how they tie together."

"That's an excellent question," remarked Ken. "We've just started implementing a Design for Six Sigma program here at Donetics within the last six months. I can relate to your comment, Brad, because there's also a lot of confusion around here as well as to how lean concepts and DFSS work together. The bottom line is that these two quality initiatives are indeed complementary and work together very well. Here's what I mean." Ken drew another sketch on the whiteboard as shown in Figure 10.1.

"You obviously recognize the lean tactical objectives that we've been discussing today, Brad," commented Ken. "But as you can see, the objectives of lean and DFSS are indeed different. Consequently the primary goal of each initiative is also different—but complementary. I would say that virtually all companies are interested in reducing cycle time as well as improving quality. But the key point in applying either lean or DFSS is to first identify the goal, and then to apply the appropriate tool set from the initiative in order to meet the goal."

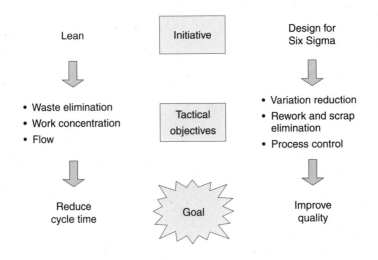

Figure 10.1   Aligning initiatives with goals.

"I see," replied Brad. "Now I understand how these initiatives work together. Thanks for clarifying that for me.

"Well, Ken, you've made quite an impression in what you've told me today," he continued. "What we've been discussing here has obviously changed the way you approach the development of your products and the procurement of your hardware."

"Without a doubt," said Ken. "It's been a significant change, but it's yielding significant results. Through our lean effort, we look at our products in a fundamentally different way. As opposed to conducting our engineering and procurement activities on a part number by part number basis, we now plan our activities on a *part family* basis.

"But our journey is not complete. Based on our success in the areas of manufacturing and product development, we're now committed to turning the entire business of Donetics into a lean enterprise. Here, take a look at this." At this point, Ken handed Brad a piece of paper containing the diagram shown in Figure 10.2.

"This is the road map we're following," continued Ken, while referring to the diagram. "As you can see, it contains

Creating a Lean Enterprise

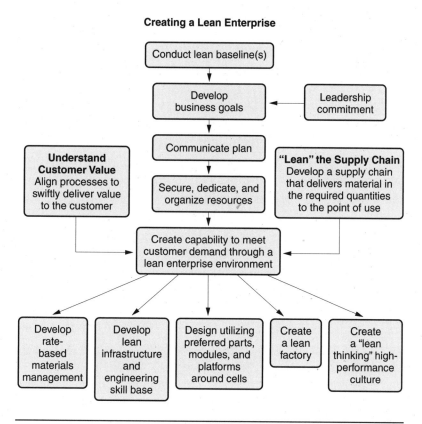

Figure 10.2 Road map to a lean enterprise.

some of the elements we've talked about today. As I mentioned, we're not finished yet, but we're well on our way."

"Very impressive," replied Brad. "I must admit, Ken, that the wheels have already started turning in my head in thinking how to apply what I've heard today to Terra Solutions."

Brad glanced at his watch.

"Well, it's getting late," he added. "Let's spend some time going over the milestones on the spring issue and then we'll call it a day. Is that okay with you?"

"Sure, Brad. But before we you that, do you mind if I turn the tables and ask you a question?" asked Ken.

"Of course not," chuckled Brad. "That's the least I can do. I've sure asked you enough questions for one day."

"What about the proposal I gave you for the new Atlas engine?" queried Ken.

"It is an unsolicited proposal," remarked Brad. "And in terms of the new engine, our initial thoughts were to go in a different direction with the electric-starting version. As I mentioned earlier, I'm visiting the supplier after I leave here to explore their product in more detail. But based on what I've heard today, I can promise you that we will give your proposal serious consideration. It's obvious that the product development strategies you described have laid the foundation for success in the future. Earlier, you talked about developing a partnership with your supply base. Well, at Terra Solutions, we're looking for the same thing from our suppliers.

"When I get back from this trip, we'll evaluate your proposal. If the preliminary analysis looks good, we can then pursue further discussions which could then lead to a formal proposal submittal."

"Fair enough," replied Ken. "That's the most I could ask for at this point. At least it's an opportunity we otherwise wouldn't have had. Okay, let's discuss those milestones. . . ."

11

The Decision

Two months later, Ken was working in his office, very preoccupied. He was anxiously awaiting a response to the Donetics proposal that had been submitted for the engine to be used on the new Atlas lawn mower. Today was the day for Terra Solutions to announce the winning proposal. Suddenly the phone rang. Ken quickly picked up the receiver and said "Good afternoon. This is Ken Hawkins."

The voice on the other end responded, "Ken. It's Brad Connelly. Look, I just wanted to call and give you the news personally. We've selected Donetics to be the engine supplier for the new Atlas lawn mower! Congratulations!"

"Wow. That's great!" replied Ken.

"Donetics put together a very good proposal," continued Brad. "As you know, you were competing against the supplier for the electric-starting engine. While both suppliers were similar in terms of technical capability and time-to-market, the key discriminator that tipped the scale in your favor was cost."

"Interesting!" replied Ken.

"As you know, Ken, we're really excited about the prospects for the new mower. And we're also excited to have you on board as a key partnering supplier for the new Atlas product. Thanks to the insight you shared with me concerning your lean product development efforts a couple of months ago, I know exactly how you'll be able to meet the aggressive commitments you outlined in your proposal."

"That's right. You do," replied Ken. "It's all about leverage. . . ."

Appendix A

Glossary

attribute—A piece of information or characteristic that describes a part in some way.

component design compliance matrix—A lean product development tool that identifies design requirements, criteria, verification and validation methods, and current experience levels for an individual component. Tool assists in developing actions when component designs do not meet minimum technical requirements.

concurrent engineering—A systematic approach to the integrated, concurrent design of products and their related processes, including manufacturing and support.

custom design—A lean product development approach that is utilized to expand the company's product portfolio. Compared against the product development continuum, the custom design approach represents the highest level of risk and lowest level of reuse.

Design for Six Sigma (DFSS)—A systematic methodology to manage and reduce variation in the product design process while meeting all customer expectations and producing products at six sigma quality levels.

lean—A philosophy of producing what is needed, when it is needed, with the minimum amount of time, resources, and space.

lean baseline event—A comprehensive self-assessment used as the starting point to initiate process improvement. The objectives of the baseline event are to identify where problems exist, shape a vision for the future, determine where to start and what to do, and to solicit management commitment to proceed with an improvement plan.

modular design—A lean product development approach that is based on using modules/subassemblies for new product design. Compared against the product development continuum, the modular design approach represents the highest level of reuse and lowest level of risk.

module—Another term for a subassembly representing high reuse potential.

multitasking—The concept of working multiple jobs concurrently. Leads to bottlenecks in the value stream and higher degrees of inefficiency and human error.

non-value-added activity—An activity that does not meet all three criteria of a value-added activity. In other words, an activity that utilizes time or resources, but does not meet the customer requirements.

part family—A grouping of parts with similar characteristics.

platform design—A lean product development approach that is based on using a platform or baseline product for a new product design. The key objective of the platform design approach is to understand and manage the technical risk.

preferred part—A "label" that is linked to a part design that is promoted for reuse. The criteria for selecting a preferred part are based on engineering, manufacturing, and business considerations unique to a specific part family.

product breakdown structure—A lean product development tool that "breaks down" a product into smaller and smaller pieces. Essentially a tree diagram starting at the product level, a product is further subdivided into major assemblies, modules/subassemblies, and finally detail parts. The key objective of this tool is to identify opportunities for part/module reuse.

product experience domain—A lean product development tool that identifies design parameters that are essential to product performance, quality, and reliability. Information can be provided in various forms including cataloged data, tables, and graphics. Tool proactively identifies risk by identifying areas where product experience exists.

technical requirements flow-down matrix—A lean product development tool that identifies product technical requirements, description, recommendations, priority, assumptions, and key affected components. When referenced against a baseline product, components affected by noncompliance are noted.

value-added activity—An activity that changes the form, fit, or function of the material/information, is done correctly the first time, and is something the customer is willing to pay for. All three criteria must be met for an activity to be considered value-added.

value stream—The sequence of all of the value-added and non-value-added activities that are necessary for producing a product.

value stream map—A lean tool that documents the sequence and flow of the activities associated with producing a product. A key objective of this tool is to aid in identifying areas of waste that represent improvement opportunities.

waste—Another term associated with non-value-added activities. Under the lean philosophy, waste can be grouped into seven different categories: defects, overproduction, inventory, motion, processing, transportation, and waiting.

Appendix B
Product Development Approach Summary

Characteristic	Product Development Approach		
	Modular Design	Platform Design	Custom Design
Key objective	Create new products through the utilization of preferred parts and modules	Create new products based on an existing baseline product	Create new products to expand the company product portfolio
Level of reuse	High	Medium	Low
Level of risk	Low	Medium	High
Level of resource requirements and process discipline	Low	Medium	High
Key data elements and tools	• Product breakdown structure • Cataloged part data • Preferred parts and modules	• Technical requirements flow-down matrix • Product experience domain • Component design compliance matrix	Leverage known data and tools as much as possible

Appendix C

Waste Examples

Type of Waste	Nonmanufacturing-Based Examples	Manufacturing-Based Examples
Defects	• Incorrect data on a form • Engineering blueprint errors	• Parts failing functional test • Part feature violating blueprint dimensional requirement
Overproduction	• Printing extra reports • Designing but never producing a product	• Machining parts with no usage requirement
Transportation	• Data handoffs • Moving a form from one department to another	• Moving parts from one machine to another
Waiting	• A form in an "in" box • Processing work on a monthly basis (closeouts, billings, and so on)	• Partially machined parts on the shop floor queued for the next operation
Inventory	• Transactions not processed • Data that is not utilized	• Finished parts that have not been purchased
Motion	• Unnecessary analysis • Extra process steps	• Extra process steps
Processing	• Approvals, sign-offs • Sending or printing files not requested	• Part inspection

Appendix D

Value Stream Map Examples

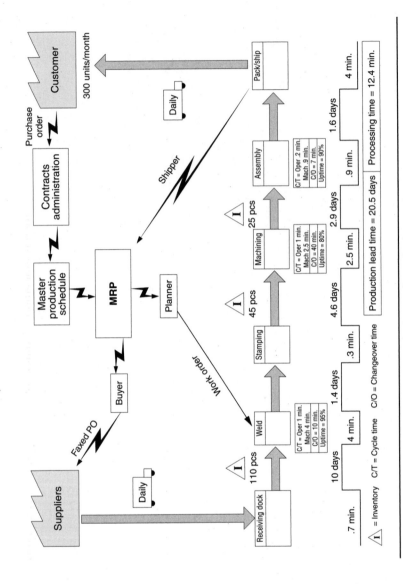

Figure D.1 Value stream map example (manufacturing).

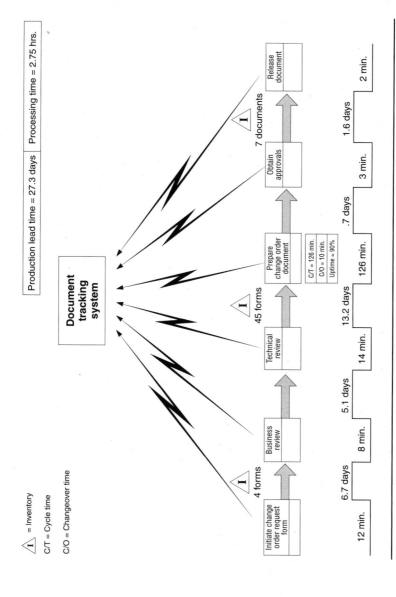

Figure D.2 Value stream map example (nonmanufacturing).

Appendix E

Common Product Development Problems

COMMON LIST OF PRODUCT DEVELOPMENT PROBLEMS IDENTIFIED IN LEAN BASELINE EVENTS

Process Issues

- Process area cluttered, disorganized

- Priorities based on "hot list," voice mail

- Metrics do not measure process outputs or desired behaviors

- Bottlenecks and excessive wait time prevalent; poor communication

- No project linkage to supplier and production process/capabilities

- Projects launched with no problem statement or clear definition

People Issues

- Technical and experience base eroding

- Practice is people-based; not process-based

- High levels of multitasking and personnel turnover

- Practitioners not colocated

- Scheduling and execution grossly dependent upon expediting, special coordination

Infrastructure and Support System Issues

- Existing product and part data unavailable

- Process continuous improvement mechanism ineffective

- Marketing and Engineering disconnected ("off-the-wall" versus "off-the-shelf")

Appendix F

Product Development Maturity Path

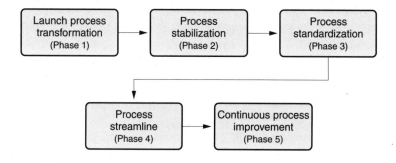

Phase 1

Launch process transformation

Purpose:
- ☑ Leadership buy-in
- ☑ Develop a plan
- ☑ Resource the plan

- ☐ Provide lean overview training for leadership team
- ☐ Train engineering leadership team
- ☐ Establish improvement expectations
- ☐ Select dedicated leader
- ☐ Develop improvement measures
- ☐ Conduct product development lean baseline event
- ☐ Identify product development critical path and value stream
- ☐ Determine and communicate process improvement vision
- ☐ Review engineering blueprint revision process performance and drivers
- ☐ Establish and resource sequenced plan to create project and information flow
- ☐ Align product development strategy to market (cycle time, cost and quality improvements)
- ☐ Align plan implementation to business strategic and operating plan

Phase 2

Process
stabilization

Purpose:
☑ Stabilize the process
☑ Focus the resources
☑ Align the culture

☐ Communicate baseline results and initial plan

☐ Identify standard process tasks

☐ Establish reuse policy and procedures for commodity-type parts

☐ Determine product and part families

☐ Implement procedures for engineering blueprint revision process stabilization

☐ Implement process quality measurement

☐ Implement design process execution measurements and visual controls

☐ Minimize identified bottlenecks

☐ Evaluate and manage work-in-process to generate flow

☐ Initiate sort, stabilize, shine, standardize, and sustain (5S) implementation

☐ Provide new-part impact training

☐ Focus critical skills and processes to minimize multitasking and changeover

☐ Facilitate lean transformation integrated through goal deployment

☐ Institute program management within the product development process

Phase 3

Purpose:

☑ Parts and product standardization

☑ Process standardization

☑ Supply chain alignment

Process standardization

❏ Define reuse architecture for product families

❏ Establish reuse policy and procedure for traditional "designed" parts

❏ Catalog part and product capability data

❏ Create modules and identify preferred parts to support reuse

❏ Create CAD models of modules/preferred parts to facilitate reuse

❏ Develop point-of-use information to support reuse philosophy

❏ Identify critical part family suppliers

❏ Develop relationships with strategic suppliers

❏ Identify standard cycle times and standard work procedures

❏ Identify standard tests, documents, tooling, and instrumentation setups

❏ Align product development process to manufacturing cells and identify process capabilities misalignments

❏ Correct obvious process bottlenecks

❏ Integrate lean thinking with job descriptions

Phase 4

| Process streamline |

Purpose:
- ☑ Supply chain rationalization
- ☑ Focus on the flow of value
- ☑ Eliminate sources of waste

☐ Maximize reuse of preferred parts and modules

☐ Identify key characteristics and align to part/process capability

☐ Verify known product capabilities through testing and analysis

☐ Streamline information flow for product development and engineering blueprint revision processes

☐ Develop point-of-use information to support flow, maximize reuse of analysis and design capability data in module, platform, and custom design approaches

☐ Develop probabilistic and sensitivity analysis methods to predict product capabilities

☐ Cross-train and colocate personnel with critical skills

☐ Implement concurrent processes wherever possible

☐ Institutionalize 5S

☐ Make process and daily performance apparent through mature visual controls

☐ Align suppliers and parts procurement to part families

Phase 5

⇨ | Continuous process improvement |

Purpose:
- ☑ Supply chain optimization
- ☑ Mature the culture
- ☑ Design for a competitive advantage

❏ Re-baseline product development process every 18 to 24 months

❏ Maintain improvement opportunities connected to business strategic and operating plan

❏ Redesign existing high-volume products to reduce cost and facilitate product flow in the factory

❏ Continue to improve information flow by automating design analysis and the selection of reuse components in product development tools

❏ Capture and utilize lessons learned; convert to best practices

❏ Connect design and product capability to business growth strategy

❏ Integrate customers and suppliers through the product development process via e-business

❏ Align processes with customer and market needs

❏ Maximize use of product development process as a competitive weapon

❏ Proactively extend product capabilities to meet market needs

References

Supplemental material on the concepts and implementation of lean approaches:

Hines, Peter, and David Taylor. *Going Lean: A Guide to Implementation.* Available from: Lean Enterprise Research Centre, Aberconway Building, Colum Drive, Cardiff CF10 3EU, UK.

Rother, Mike, and John Shook. *Learning to See: Value Stream Mapping to Add Value and Eliminate Munda.* Brookline, MA: The Lean Enterprise Institute, 1998.

Swartz, James B. *The Hunters and the Hunted: A Non-Linear Solution for Reengineering the Workplace.* New York: Productivity Press, 1994.

Taylor, David, and David Brunt. *Manufacturing Operations and Supply Chain Management: The Lean Approach.* Stamford, CT: Thomson Learning, 2001.

Womack, James P., and Daniel T. Jones. *Lean Thinking: Banish Waste and Create Wealth in your Corporation.* New York: Simon & Schuster, 1996.

Womack, James P., Daniel T. Jones, and Daniel Roos. *The Machine that Changed the World.* New York: Rawson Associates, 1990.

Index

A

attribute, 30–31, 45–46

C

cataloged data. *See* cataloging information
cataloging information, 30–32, 44–46
component design compliance matrix, 36, 40–41
concurrent engineering, 55–56
custom design, 22–23, 67
customer requirements, 22–23

D

data management, 43–47
Design for Six Sigma (DFSS), 57–58

E

enterprise resource planning (ERP) system, 30, 44

L

lean, 12
lean baseline event, 16–18
lean concepts, 12–19, 57–59
lean enterprise, 58–59
lean manufacturing principles, 12
leverage with the customer, 22–23
leveraging knowledge, 19, 22, 40

M

modular design, 25–33, 67
module, 25, 26, 27, 29
multitasking, 18–19

N

non-value-added activity, 13–14, 16

P

part family, 29–32, 51–55

Buttons for General Washington

by Peter and Connie Roop
illustrated by
Peter E. Hanson

SCHOLASTIC INC.
New York Toronto London Auckland Sydney
Mexico City New Delhi Hong Kong

For Father—a patriotic son of the American revolution whose heritage enhances our history

ISBN 0-439-27605-5

12 11 10 9 8 7 6 5 4 3 2 1   1 2 3 4 5 6/0

Printed in the U.S.A.   23

First Scholastic printing, February 2001

AUTHORS' NOTE

Spies played an important role in the Revolutionary War. American spies kept General George Washington informed about the size of British troops and the state of their supplies, and they often discovered when and where the British planned to attack.

In the fall of 1777, the British army, under the command of General Howe, had captured and occupied Philadelphia. The Darragh family lived across the street from General Howe's British headquarters. As Quakers, the Darraghs were gentle people who used "thee," "thy," and "thou" as forms of address, dressed plainly, and opposed violence. They were not supposed to fight on either side, but Charles, the oldest Darragh boy, had joined General Washington's army, and the rest of the family became spies to aid in his safety.

Mr. Darragh, a teacher, created a code for secret messages. Mrs. Darragh, who later became the most famous spy of the family, hid the messages in the buttons of her son John's coat. Fourteen-year-old John then took the messages to Washington's camp, where Charles Darragh read them.

This story tells what might have happened on one of John Darragh's dangerous missions as an American spy.

"Are any soldiers in the street, John?"
his mother asked.

"Only the guard at General Howe's
headquarters," John answered.

"Remember, John.
Keep away from the British soldiers,"
his mother said.

"And go the way I told thee."

"But I know a faster way,"
John said.

"Do as thy mother asks,"
his father said.

"She has sent messages to
General Washington before."

John nodded his head.
He wished that his mother would
finish sewing the new buttons
on his coat.
He was nervous and in a hurry
to be on his way to
General Washington's camp.

"Here, John," his mother said at last.
"The new buttons look
just like the old ones."
John took his coat.
He ran his fingers over
the cloth-covered buttons.
He could not feel the small holes
inside the buttons.
Secret messages for General Washington
were hidden in those holes.

"If I am caught, will anyone
be able to read the messages?"
John asked.
"No," answered his father.
"I wrote them in a code that
only thy brother Charles can read."
"I wish I could give the buttons
to General Washington himself,"
John said.
"Maybe someday thee will,"
his mother said.
John carefully buttoned his coat.
"Be careful," his father warned.
"The British are looking
for American spies."

"If they catch thee, it means prison—
or worse," his mother said.
A shiver ran down John's back.

He knew that captured spies
were lucky to end up in prison.
Usually they were hanged.
"I will be careful," John said.
"Here is thy pass to leave
Philadelphia," his mother said.
"Thou needs it to get
past the British guards."

John put the pass in his pocket.
His hands shook as he touched
the buttons for good luck.
"We will wait supper for thee,"
his mother said.
"Godspeed, John," his father said.

John walked up Second Street.

He turned on Market Street.

British soldiers were everywhere.

John wished they would all
go back to England.
John walked slower as he neared
the guardpost at the edge of town.

"Hey, Yankee Doodle," he heard
a voice call from behind him.
John turned quickly.
It was Samuel Baker.
Samuel's family liked
the British soldiers.
They wanted the British
to win the war.
The Bakers and other Tories
wanted America to be
part of England again.
John hated Samuel even more than
he hated the British soldiers.

"Did you see all of our new soldiers?"
Samuel asked.

"You Americans can never win now.
General Howe will whip Washington
before Christmas."

"He will not," John said fiercely.

"Oh, yes, he will," Samuel said.

"We British are too strong for you."
John stepped up to Samuel.

"Just thee wait and see who wins
the war," John said angrily.

"When we win, thee can return to
England where thou belongs!"

"Who is going to make me?"
Samuel said, poking John.

"Me!" John yelled.

Before John could move,

Samuel hit him hard in the stomach.

John fell down.

"See," Samuel said.

"We will win."

Samuel walked away proudly.

Brushing off his coat, John stood up.
He wished he could hit Samuel back,
even though he knew that
he should not fight.
Besides, he knew it was more important
to reach General Washington's camp.

John stopped at the guardpost.

A red-coated British soldier

took his pass.

He looked at it for a long time.

John began to worry.

"You are going to your aunt's house?"

the soldier asked.

"Yes," answered John.

"I must check each pass carefully,"

the soldier said.

"There are many American spies.

You are not a spy are you?"

the soldier asked with a smile.

"Oh, no, sir," John answered quickly.

"Off with you then," said the soldier.

"Just remember, we hang

any spies we catch."

Well, thou won't catch me, John thought as he put the pass back in his pocket.

John knew he should not be too
sure of himself, though,
so he kept a sharp lookout
for more British soldiers.
They might guess that he was
a spy if they found him
past his aunt's house.
They might even find
the secret messages.

25

John stopped suddenly.
He heard horses coming.
He jumped over a ditch
and hid behind a tree.

26

Five British soldiers
came along the road.
They passed slowly.
They were looking for someone.

27

John waited until the soldiers
had ridden away.
He touched his buttons for good luck.
A button was missing!
John looked all over the ground.
He could not find the button anywhere.
Then he remembered Samuel Baker's blow.
The button must have come off
near the guardhouse.
John started to run back down the road
toward Philadelphia.
His breath came in short gasps.
He had to find that button.

He stopped near the guardpost.

He looked all around for the button.

"Are you back so soon?"

John jumped in surprise.

The British guard walked toward him.

"I lost one of my buttons," John said.

"My mother would not be happy
if I could not find it."

The soldier held out his hand.

30

He had John's button!
"I found it where you boys
were fighting," the soldier said.
John tried to keep his hands from
shaking as he took the button.
He hoped the soldier
had not found the message.
"Thank thee for finding my button,"
John said, backing away.
"On your way, then," said the soldier.

John put the button
deep in his pocket.
He looked at the sky.
It was past noon.
Against his mother's warning,
he took a shortcut through the woods
toward General Washington's camp.
John stopped for a rest after an hour.
He took a long drink from an icy stream.

Suddenly, a hand grabbed him from
behind as he stood up.
"What might you be doing in these
woods?" asked a gruff voice.
John was spun around
before he could answer.
He faced a bearded man.
The man aimed a pistol at John.

John said the first words
that came to him.
"I was hunting."
"Hunting without a gun?" the man asked.
"I was really going to my aunt's house,"
John said.
"I will take you with me to find out
the truth," the man said sharply.
"Now march," he ordered.
John knew that the man would
shoot him if he tried to run.
They walked through the woods
for a long time.
John was hungry and tired.
He was scared, too.
Where was the man taking him?
What would John do
if they were going to a British camp?

At last they came to an open field.
A large white tent stood in one corner.
Soldiers in blue uniforms
were marching in the field.
It was an American camp.

John breathed a sigh of relief.
Once he talked to Charles,
everything would be all right.
"We will have the truth from you now,"
the man told John.

He took John to the white tent.
"I have a spy here," the man told
a soldier guarding the tent.
"I caught him prowling
in the woods near Philadelphia."

The soldier stepped into the tent.

He was back within a moment.

"Bring him in."

The bearded man pushed John

into the tent.

"Sit down, son,"
said a tall man in a blue uniform.
John sat in a wooden chair.
"They tell me you are a spy,"
the man said.
"You are young for a spy.
Whose side do you spy for?"
"General Washington's side," John said.
"I am John Darragh.
Charles Darragh is my brother.
He helps General Washington.
Can I see Charles now?"
The man turned to the soldier.
"Send Charles Darragh to me at once."
John sat stiffly
in front of the uniformed man.
It seemed like a year
before Charles arrived.

"Why, John," Charles said in surprise.
John smiled.
Now he could prove
that he spied for Washington.
"Mother sent me.
I have some messages
for General Washington."
John took the loose button
from his pocket.

"There is a message in Father's code
hidden inside."
Charles uncovered the button.
He took out the message
and looked at it.
"Please decode the message right away,"
the tall man said.
"Don't, Charles," said John.
"Only General Washington
is supposed to know."

Charles laughed at his brother.

"John, this *is* General Washington."

General Washington held out his hand.

John shook it.

"It is an honor to shake the hand
of so brave a patriot,"
the General said.

"Thank thee, sir," John said.

"Charles," said the General,
"please report to me after you
have decoded the messages."

General Washington left the tent.

Charles began cutting the buttons
off John's coat.
John could not believe that he
had met General Washington.
Washington's words of praise
still filled John's ears.

After removing the messages,
Charles sewed the buttons
back on John's coat.
"Now be careful on the way home,"
Charles said.
"We need thee to bring more buttons."

John touched the buttons for good luck.
Then he laughed as he put on his coat.
"I will bring enough buttons for
General Washington's whole army!"